# Oh For Crying Out Loud

## Tears of *Joy* Devotional

# Oh For Crying Out Loud

## Tears of *Joy* Devotional

### Lisa Cassman

**H**alo
PUBLISHING
INTERNATIONAL

# Halo
**PUBLISHING
INTERNATIONAL**

Halo Publishing International
7550 WIH-10 #800, PMB 2069,
San Antonio, TX 78229

First Edition, March 2024
ISBN: 978-1-63765-586-3

Halo Publishing International is a self-publishing company that publishes adult fiction and non-fiction, children's literature, self-help, spiritual, and faith-based books. We continually strive to help authors reach their publishing goals and provide many different services that help them do so. We do not publish books that are deemed to be politically, religiously, or socially disrespectful, or books that are sexually provocative, including erotica. Halo reserves the right to refuse publication of any manuscript if it is deemed not to be in line with our principles. Do you have a book idea you would like us to consider publishing? Please visit www.halopublishing.com for more information.

I dedicate this book to my mom, Evelyn Kako.

She is a great example to so many, and you can really see the joy of the Lord in her life. Her belief in God and her relationship with Him was an example that led me to the Lord. She loves all people and is nonjudgmental.

The title of this devotional came as I recalled with a smile one of her favorite sayings throughout her life: "Oh, for crying out loud!"

*Without Christ, you can't have joy. To have joy, you need to have Christ lead your life.*
*– Evelyn Kako*

# CONTENTS

# MOM'S FAVORITE SCRIPTURE

Psalm 91

(New International Version)
Whoever dwells in the shelter of the Most High
will rest in the shadow of the Almighty.
I will say of the Lord, "He is my refuge and my fortress,
my God, in whom I trust."

Surely he will save you
from the fowler's snare
and from the deadly pestilence.
He will cover you with his feathers,
and under his wings you will find refuge;
his faithfulness will be your shield and rampart.
You will not fear the terror of night,
nor the arrow that flies by day,
nor the pestilence that stalks in the darkness,
nor the plague that destroys at midday.
A thousand may fall at your side,
ten thousand at your right hand,
but it will not come near you.
You will only observe with your eyes
and see the punishment of the wicked.

If you say, "The Lord is my refuge,"
and you make the Most High your dwelling,
no harm will overtake you,
no disaster will come near your tent.
For he will command his angels concerning you
to guard you in all your ways;
they will lift you up in their hands,
so that you will not strike your foot against a stone.
You will tread on the lion and the cobra;
you will trample the great lion and the serpent.

"Because he loves me," says the Lord, "I will rescue him;
I will protect him, for he acknowledges My name.
He will call on Me, and I will answer him;
I will be with him in trouble,
I will deliver him and honor him.
With long life I will satisfy him
and show him my salvation."

# An Introductory Word

As you're doing this devotional, I'd like you to really open your heart and mind to receive the feeling of joy. You may be sad as bad things keep happening to you. Or perhaps you just can't get past something that has hindered you. Knowing that you may possess the joy of the Lord can and will change your perspective on life.

Only you can change your attitude toward what or how something has happened. Don't let your life go by without knowing that God can and will get you through every season.

Keep your focus on the truth, and you will be set free. Great and mighty things will come to you from God.

At eighteen, I asked for a Bible as my graduation gift. This is the verse Mom wrote inside the cover. It has brought me through a lot in my life.

*Call unto me, and I will answer thee, and show thee*
*great and mighty things, which thou knowest not.*
*–Jeremiah 33:3 (King James Version)*

# DAY 1

*Shout for joy to the Lord, all the earth.*
*Worship the Lord with gladness;*
*come before him with joyful songs.*
*–Psalm 100:1–2*

Do you feel pressured to go to church? Do you feel that life has thrown you a bummer of a hand, and it's hard to praise God? We are told to make a joyful noise. Whether it is in private or in a church building full of others praising Him—Scripture doesn't say where you have to pray—just come before Him with joyful songs.

Even if your life takes a turn for the worst, you can still sing to God. It may not be easy, but He will give you peace and joy in your heart as you praise Him. Put on your favorite worship song, and just bask in His presence. Feel the joy that you so desire and long for.

## Challenge for Today

Write down some of your favorite songs, and listen to one that will inspire you. Then take a moment to jot down the things you appreciate about going to church.

## Prayer

God, help me see the joy You bring into our lives. Help me to see that no matter what comes my way, You will always be there, and You will bring joy into my heart. I want to open up my whole being to You and receive it today.

# DAY 2

*But let all who take refuge in you be glad;*
*let them ever sing for joy.*
*Spread your protection over them,*
*that those who love your name may rejoice in you.*
*—Psalm 5:11*

Don't hide your love for God. Take it with you wherever you go. Don't think about the things that you haven't gotten answers for; thank Him for what He has done for you and what He is going to do for you. Those who love Him will spread His love to everyone around them.

We make choices sometimes to do things that we shouldn't do, but He still loves us and wants what is best. Keep moving in His word and in His name, and rejoice!

## Challenge for Today

Find your favorite place, spend some time with God, and ask Him to show you whom you need to reach out to. Make a list of those you can contact and check in with today. What are some things He has done in your life that you can share with others?

## Prayer

God, I want to listen to Your voice so I know whom I can reach out to. Help me to listen to Your voice and be the example that I should be so others can rejoice in Your name. Protect me and those around me. Help us all to be the best examples that we can be.

# DAY 3

*The Lord has done it this very day;*
*let us rejoice today and be glad.*
*–Psalm 118:24*

This is the day the Lord has made—today and every day. The sunrise occurs in the morning. Maybe you don't witness it every day, but the morning starts with you waking up and seeing the beauty in what has been given to you.

You are loved unconditionally, and everything that happens to you will eventually make you stronger. Just put your trust in God, and know that He has made each day for you.

Today is a new beginning for you. Look to the One who has created you and all the things around you, including this day for you.

## Challenge for Today

Watch the sunrise the next chance you get, or even just witness the world as it lightens outside. Close your eyes, and talk to God. Open your eyes slowly, and thank Him for all the beauty.

## Prayer

God, help me to see Your beauty each day, knowing that things may not be as I had planned, but that Your plans are better than mine. I will trust You today, knowing

that You will help me through this day. Take my hand,
Lord, and walk with me down the road of life.

_____

_____

_____

_____

_____

_____

_____

_____

_____

_____

_____

_____

_____

_____

# DAY 4

*Lord, you understand;*
*remember me and care for me.*
*Avenge me on my persecutors.*
*You are long-suffering—do not take me away;*
*Think of how I suffer reproach for your sake.*
*When your words came, I ate them;*
*they were my joy and my heart's delight,*
*for I bear your name,*
*Lord God Almighty.*
*–Jeremiah 15:15–16*

Do you sometimes feel no one understands you or cares for you? You may be having that kind of day, but God's Word says that He cares for you. God has shown His love many times over to you and those around you.

Where is your heart today? Do you delight in Him? Do you feel joy at the mention of His name? Are your words disappointing or rejoicing? Are you trusting in Him?

## Challenge for Today

What has God done for you that gives you instant joy in your heart just thinking about it? Thank Him for it again right now. How do you know that God is real and that He cares for you? Do you feel Him in your heart?

## Prayer

God, help me feel joy and delight in Your name. I want my heart to see You for who You are and not what I think You are. Help my heart be open to Your presence; fill my mouth with Your words that I can share with others.

# DAY 5

*Nehemiah said, "Go and enjoy choice food and sweet drinks, and send some to those who have nothing prepared. This day is holy to our Lord. Do not grieve, for the joy of the LORD is your strength."*
*–Nehemiah 8:10*

Have you ever lived through a time when you didn't have anything to eat or drink in your home? Have you known someone who may have needed a little extra help, and though you felt God nudging you, you didn't do anything because you thought that they would receive aid elsewhere?

God wants us to help those in need because they are His children. Some are too ashamed to ask for help; be obedient, and don't take that for granted. Where is your heart today? Are you open to receiving as well as giving help?

God is good all the time; He wants what is best for all of us.

# Challenge for Today

Pray and make a list of the people you know who may be needing a little something extra right now. What can you do to help them? What can you do to bring a little joy into their lives?

# Prayer

Lord, I ask you to show me today someone in need whom I may be able to reach out to. Help me to see them even if they are too ashamed to ask for anything. Allow my heart to be open and not bitter or judgmental in any way.

_____

_____

_____

_____

_____

_____

_____

_____

_____

_____

_____

_____

_____

_____

_____

# DAY 6

*I keep my eyes always on the Lord.*
*With Him at my right hand, I will not be shaken.*

*Therefore my heart is glad, and my tongue rejoices;*
*my body also will rest secure,*
*because You will not abandon me to the realm of the dead,*
*nor will You let your faithful one see decay.*
*—Psalm 16:8–10*

None of us is perfect, but we need to strive to live the best we can for the Lord, keeping our eyes on Him. If you stumble and fall, pick yourself back up; remember it is a new day. God is always with you.

Life can and will throw us for a loop, but that loop doesn't have to break us. Stay strong, and pull yourself through.

Are your eyes on God or the things that can take you down?

## Challenge for Today

Look up the song "Rejoice in the Lord Always." Sing along with it, and just bask in His presence.

Are there any things trying to pull you down? Write them down along with what can help you get back up again.

## Prayer

God, help me to remember that You are the one who keeps me going. Allow my heart to be open, and grant me the certainty that even on a bad day, I can rejoice in what You have done for me and know that You will continue to bring me through. My body rests in You, so I don't have to feel weak.

_____

_____

_____

_____

_____

_____

_____

_____

_____

_____

_____

_____

_____

_____

_____

# DAY 7

*You make known to me the path of life;*
*You will fill me with joy in Your presence,*
*with eternal pleasures at Your right hand.*
*—Psalm 16:11*

What is better than the feeling of joy we have in knowing the Lord here on earth? Knowing that our eternal life will be so much more beautiful than all the beauty He's already given us here on earth.

It's right around the corner. We should be prepared to live each day as if it is our last day on earth. Live to celebrate life. Don't live to die or have an attitude of impending doom. Make each day you are still alive a day of rejoicing.

Remember the feeling you experienced when you gave your life to Him. Keep that in your heart each day.

Do you feel the joy of the Lord in your heart?

## Challenge for Today

Take a moment, and ask Him to forgive and cleanse you. Have a new heart, and become a new creation in Him.

Each day, can you feel the joy of His presence? Knowing He is the one who will take you home with Him soon, write some thoughts on your feelings.

# Prayer

Lord, I ask You to come into my heart and cleanse me. I want to live my life for You. Help me to renew myself each day for a newness in You. I want a reason to live here on earth while experiencing the joy of knowing I will be with You eternally.

_____

_____

_____

_____

_____

_____

_____

_____

_____

_____

_____

_____

# DAY 8

*For his anger lasts only a moment,*
*but his favor lasts a lifetime;*
*weeping may stay for the night,*
*but rejoicing comes in the morning.*
*—Psalm 30:5*

Are you having a bad day? Moment? Week? Maybe you have felt sad or angry for a while. Maybe someone has hurt you, and you can't forgive them. What has you down?

We sometimes allow life to get in the way of our feelings. It doesn't have to last a lifetime or even an entire day. This verse tells us that when you start to feel as if the night is long, it doesn't have to last forever because joy comes when you wake up in the morning.

# Challenge for Today

Close your eyes, take a deep breath, and have a moment with God. Feel His presence, and thank Him for the feeling of joy.

Sometimes, we allow life events to get to us. Write down some things that have gotten you down. How can you change your attitude?

# Prayer

Lord, thank You for the joy that comes in the morning. I don't have to hang on to all that upsets me. Help me to forgive those who have hurt me and to change my attitude toward them and the situation.

I want to live my life completely for You, not for the world and what it has brought me.

_____

_____

_____

_____

_____

_____

_____

_____

_____

_____

_____

_____

_____

_____

_____

# DAY 9

*You turned my wailing into dancing;*
*you removed my sackcloth*
*and clothed me with joy.*
*—Psalm 30:11*

What has caused you to cry? Is it something small, or is it a major life event? Is it pain? Maybe someone has hurt you. Are you holding in your tears and trying to stay strong? For whom are you staying strong?

It is okay to cry. Crying is good for you in a time of sadness. Think about the pain Jesus endured on the cross, and think about the pain we cause every day.

The sackcloth was made from goat hair, and it was worn while mourning. Are you mourning today? Take off your sackcloth, and put on joy. Allow others to know the joy of Christ through your example.

## Challenge for Today

What made you start wearing the sackcloth? Are you ready to take it off?

Today, wear colorful clothes to signify to yourself that you are celebrating the joy of the Lord that is always available to you.

# Prayer

Lord, help me turn the mourning in my life into dancing. Show me what to wear in Your honor today so that I can feel true joy in You.

I ask for a new love and a new viewpoint about what is going on around me in my life. I want to keep steadfast in Your word.

_____

_____

_____

_____

_____

_____

_____

_____

_____

_____

_____

# DAY 10

*Clap your hands, all you nations;*
*shout to God with cries of joy.*
*—Psalm 47:1*

*Take delight in the Lord,*
*and He will give you the desires of your heart.*
*—Psalm 37:4*

Life can and will get us down. How can we change our attitude? Shout to God, all the earth. Are you telling others about who God is? He states in this Scripture that we are to clap our hands and shout to Him.

Delighting in the Lord to receive the desires of our hearts doesn't mean He will give us everything we want. We can sometimes be selfish and ask for things we don't need. God loves us so much that he often gives us our desires, yet He knows what is best for us. He also gives us peace, joy, understanding, and other feelings we long for.

## Challenge for Today

What are some things that you asked God for, but instead of receiving what you asked for, He answered and provided what was best for you? What feelings are you longing to experience in your life today?

## Prayer

Lord, I ask for Your help with my attitude and ask for love, joy, understanding, and peace in my life. I ask for Your will to be done, not my own. Help me to trust that Your way is best, so even when I don't receive what I hoped for, I will still shout Your name out, declaring

that You are God all the time and know what I need.
I believe it is for the best when You answer me.

_____

_____

_____

_____

_____

_____

_____

_____

_____

_____

_____

_____

_____

_____

_____

_____

# DAY 11

*Consider it pure joy, my brothers and sisters, whenever you face trials of many kinds, because you know that the testing of your faith produces perseverance.*
*–James 1:2–3*

*In Him our hearts rejoice,*
*for we trust in His holy name.*
*–Psalm 33:21*

The Bible tells us to "consider it pure joy" when we face trials. It is understood that life isn't perfect, but it is your reaction that matters. It can be a challenge to feel good about yourself or a situation when something difficult happens. Do you trust God enough to know that He will see you through it, to know that He is not the one who causes bad things to happen?

He loves you too much. He wants what is best for you because of His unconditional love. God will never leave you or forsake you. When you have complete trust in God, you can get past trials of any kind. People will let us down, but God will not.

## Challenge for Today

Where is your faith today? What has happened that, instead of blaming God for the situation, it made you realize you needed to "consider it pure joy"? Has someone hurt you, and you know you need to get past the hurt they caused?

## Prayer

Lord, I ask You to help me see the joy in all that happens. Help me not to pick and choose when to trust You. I know that things can happen to make me feel hurt, and that is okay. I want to trust You completely and unconditionally, to know that You will help me through everything. I want to trust You more than anything that has happened or will happen.

_____

_____

_____

_____

_____

_____

_____

_____

_____

_____

_____

_____

_____

_____

# DAY 12

*Restore to me the joy of your salvation
and grant me a willing spirit, to sustain me.*

*Then I will teach transgressors your ways,
so that sinners will turn back to you.
Deliver me from the guilt of bloodshed, O God,
you who are God my Savior,
and my tongue will sing of your righteousness.*
*–Psalm 51:12–14*

Are you living an example, so others can and will come to God? Do you want to teach others God's ways? When others see the joy in you, they can also look to the Lord and have the same joy you have.

Going through valleys is not fun or easy, but when you get to the top of the mountain, you can see what He does for you. Keep your head high, and don't give up. Do you need to restore your joy and sing of His righteousness?

## Challenge for Today

Ask God to help you get through the guilt you feel in your life. Write about what it is you need to get through.

Can you think of someone whom you can reach out to who needs to know the Lord? How about someone you need to forgive or ask to forgive you?

## Prayer

Lord, I ask you to help me keep the joy that I need to teach others about Your love and to be an example so that they can sing of Your righteousness. I want a willing spirit so that I can rejoice in You. Help me to be the best that I can so others see the truth through me.

# DAY 13

*My lips will shout for joy
when I sing praise to you —
I whom you have delivered.*
—Psalm 71:23

*Rejoice in the Lord and be glad, you righteous;
sing, all you who are upright in heart!*
—Psalm 32:11

Have you been delivered from evil? Have you used your lips to shout and sing His praises? It is okay to have a bad day, a temporary bad attitude, but don't forget who holds you and holds your future.

God knows your heart and your every move. He can take your shredded heart and set you free. Nothing is ever so bad that you can't praise Him in the midst of it. He doesn't want to be pushed away.

The path you take will determine where you go and your attitude of joy. Remember all his wonderful works in your life and in the lives of others, past and present.

## Challenge for Today

What is something that you can change within yourself to help you get through the day?

Will you have to change your way of thinking or just keep going in the direction you were?

## Prayer

Lord, help me to take my heart and give it all to You to make it whole so I can have the joy and understanding that I so long for and desire. Thank You for Your love, for delivering me from evil, and for giving me the strength to shout out Your praises.

_____

_____

_____

_____

_____

_____

_____

_____

_____

_____

_____

_____

_____

_____

# DAY 14

*The Lord is my strength and my shield;*
*my heart trusts in him, and he helps me.*
*My heart leaps for joy,*
*and with my song I praise him.*
*–Psalm 28:7*

*Because you are my help,*
*I sing in the shadow of your wings.*
*I cling to you;*
*your right hand upholds me.*
*–Psalm 63 :7–8*

Do you feel weak and need strength? Do you go to the world or to God for help? Many times, we look to worldly things for protection and help. Do you want the shadow cast over you to be from God, and the world to hold you and comfort you? Comfort should come from God, who loves us and has done so much for us. He is great and mighty.

At times, we feel we need someone to hold us when we should look to Him. Choose God; He wants you to have the freedom to trust Him. He will hold you and comfort you.

## Challenge for Today

What or whom will you choose to comfort you and give you strength? Will you take the worldly shortcut, or will you go to God for help? Can you accept the freedom He offers?

## Prayer

Lord, please help me to understand that You are the only true way to receive comfort and to know that You will always be there to hold me when I feel alone. I want to accept You as my strength and shield. You alone can protect me and love me unconditionally. I now understand You will not hurt me.

_____

_____

_____

_____

_____

_____

_____

_____

_____

_____

_____

_____

_____

_____

_____

_____

# Day 15

*A wise son brings joy to his father,*
*but a foolish man despises his mother.*

*Folly brings joy to one who has no sense,*
*but whoever has understanding keeps a straight course.*

*Plans fail for lack of counsel,*
*but with many advisers they succeed.*

*A person finds joy in giving an apt reply—*
*and how good is a timely word!*

*The path of life leads upward for the prudent*
*to keep them from going down to the realm of the dead.*

*The Lord tears down the house of the proud,*
*but he sets the widow's boundary stones in place.*
*—Proverbs 15:20–25*

Have you had someone approach you to talk about someone else, and then you took the bait and proceeded to talk about them also? We as humans tend to say things we shouldn't say. We know we shouldn't be negative about others, but we do it to fit in, or just because we're unhappy with ourselves.

We should be staying positive about others, knowing God has given us a new life. Watch your tongue. Tell yourself you are a Bible-believing, Jesus-loving person who should live like Him. Would Jesus say the things that you are saying, and would He approve of the language coming from your mouth?

## Challenge for Today

About whom have you said things that you need to make it right? Do you have impure thoughts going through your mind that can take away your trust in God?

## Prayer

Lord, please help me to have pure thoughts. Help me to be the example that You want me to be. Show me the right words to say so I can be the best example for others to see the joy in me, which comes from You. I want to be wise in Your words.

# DAY 16

After a long time, the master of those servants returned
and settled accounts with them. The man who had
received five bags of gold brought the other five.
"Master," he said, "you entrusted me with five bags
of gold. See, I have gained five more."

His master replied, "Well done, good and faithful
servant! You have been faithful with a few things;
I will put you in charge of many things. Come and
share your master's happiness!"
–Matthew 25:19–21

Keep on doing God's work. Work hard; don't quit. Have you slowed down or slacked off? Work diligently and with a joyful heart. Do you feel overwhelmed and as if you're not getting anything from life? Do it all for God.

Your attitude can change the way you feel about work. Life can change your attitude and the way you perceive it.

Take a moment to feel God's presence, and ask him to help you through this rough patch. Take a short break, but don't give up. Know your limits, and trust God to get you through.

## Challenge for Today

What have you done that God has said to you, "Well done, good and faithful servant"?

What is something you're doing that may make you tired and weary?

## Prayer

Lord, I want to do Your work. Help me to be faithful and true to You, to do the works You have asked me to, not just out of duty but out of faithfulness.

Thank You for trusting me to do the work and for loving me enough to keep moving forward with what You want of me. Show me what You would like me to do.

_____

_____

_____

_____

_____

_____

_____

_____

_____

_____

_____

_____

_____

_____

# Day 17

*I tell you that in the same way there will be more rejoicing in heaven over one sinner who repents than over ninety-nine righteous persons who do not need to repent.*

*Or suppose a woman has ten silver coins and loses one. Doesn't she light a lamp, sweep the house, and search carefully until she finds it? And when she finds it, she calls her friends and neighbors together and says, "Rejoice with me; I have found my lost coin." In the same way, I tell you, there is rejoicing in the presence of the angels of God over one sinner who repents.*
–Luke 15:7–10

We should rejoice when a sinner comes home, when he or she gives their life to the Lord. But, instead, we might be judgmental and see that person only for the wrong they may have done. We might look at them as if they can't change and will never live for the Lord. "But he has done so much sinning," we might think.

We are not to judge, but to rejoice as they have repented with an open and sincere heart. God loves all of us the same. We just need to realize that He doesn't like the sin, but He loves us, the sinners, anyway. Know that God is waiting with open arms.

# Challenge for Today

Look into your heart, and see if you have been judgmental about someone whom has recently given their life to Christ. Do you have something that you need to change and give to the Lord?

# Prayer

Lord, I ask You today to open my heart and help me to see the beauty in others. Help me not to judge what they have done before. I ask You to forgive me and open my heart to what You have for me. I want to live for You.

# DAY 18

*As the Father has loved me, so have I loved you. Now remain in my love. If you keep my commands, you will remain in my love, just as I have kept my Father's commands and remain in his love. I have told you this so that my joy may be in you and that your joy may be complete. My command is this: Love each other as I have loved you.*
*–John 15:9–12*

We know that God loves us. Can you love others as He loves you? His love is unconditional; ours is not perfect. We may say that we love unconditionally, but we still set conditions for those whom we love. We try our best, and still we fail. But don't let that get you down; keep your head up, and keep going forward.

God commands us to remain in love. He knows our heart and wants us to have the joy He brings us.

## Challenge for Today

Read Exodus 20 and write down the Ten Commandments.

What do they mean to you? What do you think needs to change in your heart for you to follow each one?

## Prayer

Lord, I ask You to help me to keep Your commands and Commandments. I want to live my best for You and what You have asked of me. Take my heart and life today, and help me love others as You have loved them and me.

# DAY 19

*So with you: Now is your time of grief, but I will see you again, and you will rejoice, and no one will take away your joy. In that day you will no longer ask Me anything. Very truly I tell you, my Father will give you whatever you ask in My name. Until now, you have not asked for anything in My name. Ask and you will receive, and your joy will be complete.*
*–John 16:22–24*

What a glorious day that will be when my Jesus I shall see! Know that I will see you again if you are living for the Lord.

While you may grieve for the death of a loved one, we will see them again. Nobody can take the joy away from your knowing that you will be reunited in heaven. Imagine the day when you see those lost loved ones before you and see Jesus face-to-face. No more sorrows, no more tears. Rejoice in Him.

## Challenge for Today

Write a list of those whom you miss and will see again someday.

If you could stand before Jesus right now, what would you ask Him?

## Prayer

Jesus, I thank You for the chance to see loved ones again someday. I am looking forward to the day I will see You face-to-face and know that I have done my best to live here on earth as an example of Your love to others. Thank You for Your loving arms that hold me, and thank You for showing me the truth.

# DAY 20

*…but we also glory in our sufferings, because we know that suffering produces perseverance; perseverance, character; and character, hope. And hope does not put us to shame, because God's love has been poured out into our hearts through the Holy Spirit, who has been given to us.*
*–Romans 5:3–5*

Even in the midst of pain and suffering, we know that God is shaping us. He is never finished working on us or inside of us.

God created us in His image, and yet He isn't done with us. Just as the potter molds the clay, He is continually forming us. We all have flaws, but God looks at us and knows we are wonderfully made. He never gives up on us; He knows who He has created us to be.

## Challenge for Today

Write down some things that you find positive about yourself. Look in the mirror, and tell yourself you are fearfully and wonderfully made.

## Prayer

God, thank You for making me who I am. Help me to see the beauty in Your creation and to always see the beauty in others. I understand that You are not finished with me yet, and I will continue to see that. My life is in Your hands.

# DAY 21

*Not only is this so, but we also boast in God through our Lord Jesus Christ, through whom we have now received reconciliation.*
*—Romans 5:11*

What is your relationship with God? His word says to rejoice in it. Love your God with everything you have, with your whole heart. Be proud of what you have with Him. Remember, when you plant that seed, it's okay to let someone else water and harvest it.

You can definitely be the example without being pushy and turning others away from God. Live your life, and share what you have received.

# Challenge for Today

Think of some people who might be ready to have a seed of faith planted.

What can you do to live your life as an example, so others will want what you have?

# Prayer

God, I ask You to help me to be humble, but yet an example. Let those around me see the truth in my life and want what I have. Let them come to You and find the life that they long for. Help me not to be pushy or over-bearing, but sense by Your Holy Spirit when someone is ready to hear Your gospel.

# Day 22

*Be joyful in hope, patient in affliction,*
*faithful in prayer. Share with the Lord's*
*people who are in need. Practice hospitality.*

*Bless those who persecute you;*
*bless and do not curse.*
*Rejoice with those who rejoice;*
*mourn with those who mourn.*
*–Romans 12:12–15*

There is always hope! No matter what has happened or what will happen. Stay faithful in your prayer life. Know that you will be persecuted because of your faith. Don't underestimate the power of what God has for you. Life may seem as if there isn't anything good happening, but there is always something to be thankful for. These verses say so much, and yet we don't always understand what they mean for us.

## Challenge for Today

Take these verses, and explain in your own words what they mean to you.

How can you use these in your everyday life?

## Prayer

God, please help me to understand Your words. Help me to know that others may not understand what has come in my life. Yet You are always there with me, even in the times I feel alone. Thank You for holding me and listening to my heart.

# DAY 23

*You became imitators of us and of the Lord, for you welcomed the message in the midst of severe suffering with the joy given by the Holy Spirit.*
*–1 Thessalonians 1:6*

*May the God of hope fill you with all joy and peace as you trust in him, so that you may overflow with hope by the power of the Holy Spirit.*
*–Romans 15:13*

Be an imitator of God, and welcome His beautiful message and Spirit into your life. Feel the peace and joy you so long for. Is it easy? Not always, but we can know that God is in control of every situation. Trust in Him.

We don't have to trust all people, but know that God always wants what is best for you. Trust God more than man or anything that could possibly hinder you from trusting Him.

Listen to the Holy Spirit talk to you.

## Challenge for Today

What kind of suffering have you had to endure? Have you had medical issues, financial problems, or other disappointments?

Talk to God about how you want to trust Him through it all.

## Prayer

Holy Spirit, talk to me. Allow me to hear from You what I need to hear. I want to follow You and be an imitator of You. I want the words to help others see what You have for me. Thank You for loving me and knowing what is best in my life.

_____

_____

_____

_____

_____

_____

_____

_____

_____

_____

_____

_____

_____

_____

# DAY 24

*For the kingdom of God is not a matter of eating
and drinking, but of righteousness,
peace, and joy in the Holy Spirit.*
—Romans 14:17

We sometimes take comfort in material things, whether it is clothing, food, or certain drinks. Even our job can be a material comfort. When we are stressed, it may cause us to find comfort in the things that don't really give us true comfort, only temporary relief for our mind and body.

Yes, we need to eat and drink to keep ourselves alive, but we should not overindulge or find our comfort in eating and drinking. It can be unhealthy and take away the peace and joy He means for us to experience.

## Challenge for Today

What have you found comfort in that may be unhealthy?

What can you do to change your habits?

## Prayer

Lord, I ask You to take my mind and body and help me get rid of the things that are keeping me from having joy in my life from You. I want to give myself totally and completely to You. Thank You for giving me peace and joy in my life.

# DAY 25

*…fixing our eyes on Jesus, the pioneer and perfecter of faith. For the joy set before Him, He endured the cross, scorning its shame, and sat down at the right hand of the throne of God.*
*–Hebrews 12:2*

You are running the race; perseverance has gotten you to where you are. You have practiced and worked out to gain your strength. You feel the adrenaline to push you across the finish line, but then a barrier is raised, and you don't get to cross the finish line.

Jesus has finished the race for us. He died on the cross, so we can fix our eyes on Him.

Hold your arms out; run into His. You may encounter hurdles and setbacks, but know that you can always go back. He will be waiting for you. Nobody can stop you except you.

## Challenge for Today

What have been some of the hurdles between you and the finish line with Jesus?

What can you do differently in your life to remove the hurdles?

## Prayer

Lord, I thank You for what You did on the cross. I am so sorry I haven't lived my life the way I should. I know I hurt You daily, but I want to change my life to follow

You and live the best example I know how. Thank You for the joy in knowing You.

_____

_____

_____

_____

_____

_____

_____

_____

_____

_____

_____

_____

_____

_____

# DAY 26

*Rejoice always, pray continually,*
*give thanks in all circumstances;*
*for this is God's will for you*
*in Christ Jesus.*
*–1 Thessalonians 5:16–18*

God's word says to pray continually, rejoice always, and give thanks in all circumstances. Not just sometimes, but all the time. This is God's will for you. Rejoice in all you do. Praise Him for unanswered prayers, believe healing is coming, and thank Him for what He hasn't done for us yet.

Jesus has done so much for us by answering prayers. Also, knowing what is best for us, He's done so much for us by leaving some prayed-for desires unrealized.

## Challenge for Today

What are some of your unanswered prayers?

What are some of your answered prayers?

## Prayer

Lord, thank You for answering prayers with what is best for me. I don't want to question Your will. Forgive me for my doubts. You know what is best for me, and I thank You for that.

# DAY 27

*But the fruit of the Spirit is love, joy, peace,*
*forbearance, kindness, goodness,*
*faithfulness, gentleness, and self-control.*
*Against such things there is no law.*
*–Galatians 5:22–23*

*Therefore, if you have any encouragement from being*
*united with Christ, if any comfort from his love, if*
*any common sharing in the Spirit, if any tenderness*
*and compassion, then make my joy complete by being*
*like-minded, having the same love, being one in spirit*
*and of one mind.*
*–Philippians 2:1–2*

The fruits of the spirit are things we can learn to cultivate in our life. They all work together as good for us. The verses clearly tell us to live like Christ and by the fruits of His spirit. He is gentle, kind, faithful, and so much more. He loves us unconditionally and helps us even on our worst days. Are you allowing Him to help you through the fruits of the spirit?

Be like-minded, as He has told us, and keep yourself from hatred, slander, and false accusations of others. Love as the Lord has loved you. Take comfort in His love, and remember the fruits of the spirit.

# Challenge for Today

Which fruits of the spirit resonate with you the most?

Which ones do you have the hardest time cultivating in your life?

# Prayer

Lord, thank You for the fruits of the spirit. With these in mind, You have given me a guide to live by; help me to grow them in my life. Help me to be like-minded with You, Lord, and give me the ability to see others through Your eyes.

# DAY 28

*Therefore, my brothers and sisters, you whom
I love and long for, my joy and crown,
stand firm in the Lord in this way, dear friends!*
*–Philippians 4:1*

*Rejoice in the Lord always. I will say it again: Rejoice!
Let your gentleness be evident to all. The Lord is near.
Do not be anxious about anything, but in every
situation, by prayer and petition, with thanksgiving,
present your requests to God. And the peace of God,
which transcends all understanding, will guard your
hearts and your minds in Christ Jesus.*
*–Philippians 4:4–7*

Keep your focus on positive things. We tend to dwell on the negative and question our entire life's journey when things don't go our way. It is our reaction that can take us down.

His word says not to be anxious, but to rejoice! Pray with thanksgiving, and present your requests to God.

## Challenge for Today

Thank God for what He's done for you. Write it all down.

Ask God to help you with your anxiety about any issues that you might have in your life today.

What are your prayer requests? What have you been hanging on to?

## Prayer

God, I ask You to take away my anxiety. I want to trust You with all I have, and I don't want to worry about anything. I want to change my perspective on life and know that, anything that happens, I can and will get through life's challenges.

# Day 29

*Though you have not seen Him, you love him; and even though you do not see Him now, you believe in Him and are filled with an inexpressible and glorious joy, for you are receiving the end result of your faith, the salvation of your souls.*
*–1 Peter 1:8–9*

Where is your faith? Is it wavering? Do you see wind and air? No, but you know it is there. You don't have to see God to know He is there. You can feel Him and His anointing. The more time you spend talking to Him, the more you can feel Him.

Life can throw you a curveball, but know that when you spend time with Him, you learn to trust Him more.

## Challenge for Today

What can you do to spend more time with God?

When you spend time with Him, how do you feel? Have you felt His presence?

## Prayer

God, I thank You for Your presence and the love that I can feel from You even though I can't see You. I know You are always with me. Help me to believe You are here, and then I won't feel overwhelmed. Thank You for filling me with joy!

# DAY 30

*But rejoice inasmuch as you participate*
*in the sufferings of Christ, so that you may be*
*overjoyed when His glory is revealed.*
*–1 Peter 4:13*

Life can hurt. Events or people can hurt you, but there is always a way to move forward.

Find someone who has been in the same situation and gotten through it, so you can have someone to talk to who understands, but who can also remind you that the story isn't over yet.

There are better days ahead. Also, know that what you pull through will make you stronger. It's okay to feel sad, hurt, or disappointed, but know that God is there to help you along.

# Challenge for Today

What has made you feel sad or disappointed lately?

What did you do to pull through?

# Prayer

God, You are my strength even when I feel weak. I rejoice in You and Your healing. You are my shining light even on the darkest, cloudiest day. My life is in Your hands.

# DAY 31

*That which was from the beginning, which we have heard, which we have seen with our eyes, which we have looked at and our hands have touched—this we proclaim concerning the Word of life. The life appeared; we have seen it and testify to it, and we proclaim to you the eternal life, which was with the Father and has appeared to us. We proclaim to you what we have seen and heard, so that you also may have fellowship with us. And our fellowship is with the Father and with His Son, Jesus Christ. We write this to make our joy complete.*
*—1 John 1:1–4*

Are you a walking example of who Christ is? Do others see the love you have for Him?

When someone has given their life to Christ, are you excited? Or do you judge them by their past? It is not for us to judge others for the love they have for the Lord. We have to believe every person is sincere and continue to pray for them.

Rejoice in the Lord for the sinners that have come home.

## Challenge for Today

Have you judged someone who has given their life to the Lord? Think of that person, and ask God to forgive you. Commit to praying for them going forward.

## Prayer

Lord, I ask You to help me be nonjudgmental and help me to see that I can't be judging those who have changed for You. I want to live the best I can for You and to be loving to others.

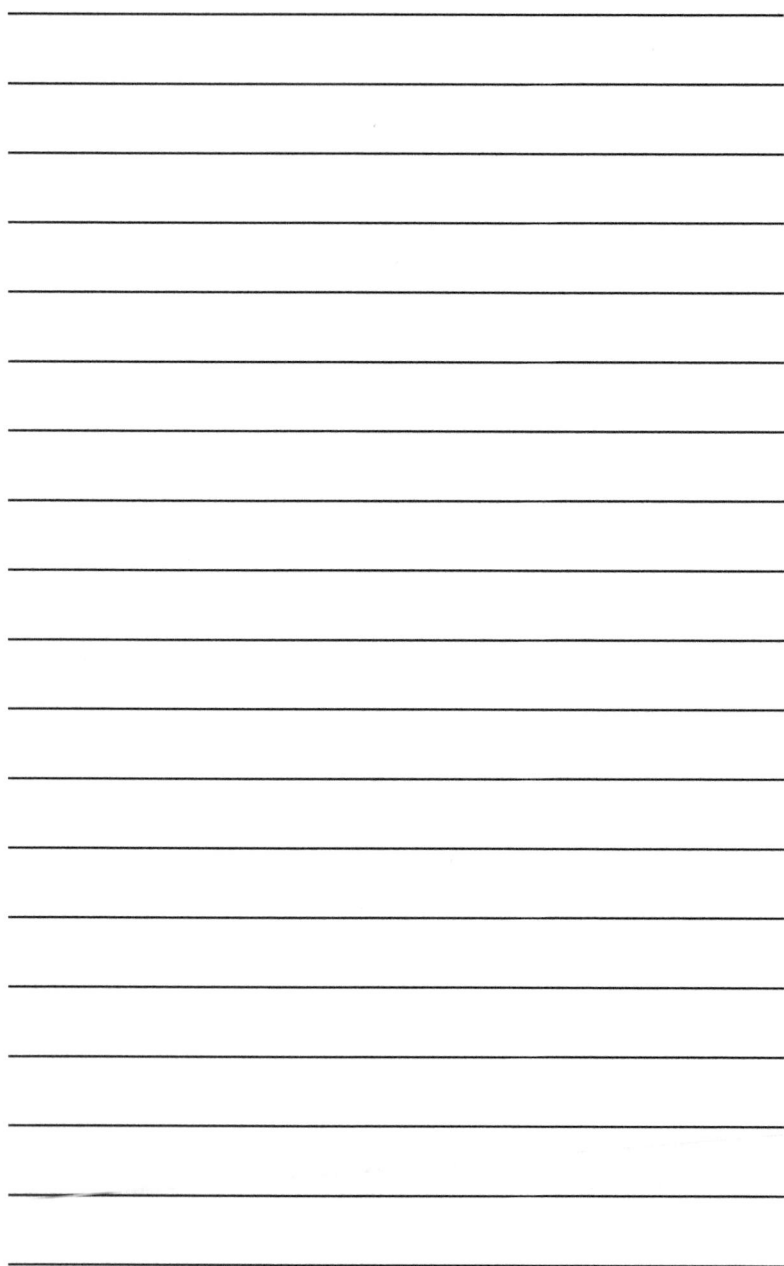

Please know that if you've read the words of this book, or any of my books, I've prayed for you and asked Him to strengthen your faith and your walk with Him. Thank you for letting me be a part of your journey with God.

I also have seven previously published titles that can be found on Amazon or via my website. I'd love to share with you

I love to hear from my readers.

God bless you, dear reader!

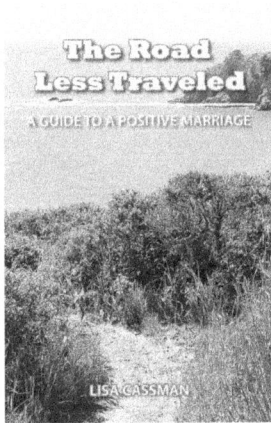

The Road Less Traveled:
A Guide to a Positive Marriage
ISBN Paperback: 978-1-61244-502-1

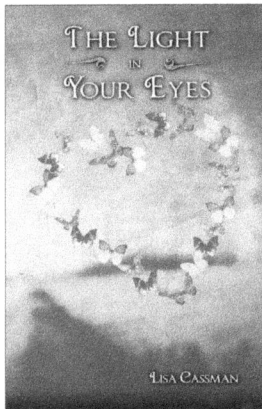

The Light in Your Eyes
ISBN Paperback: 978-1-61244-304-1

Finding the Beautiful You
ISBN Paperback: 978-1-61244-601-1

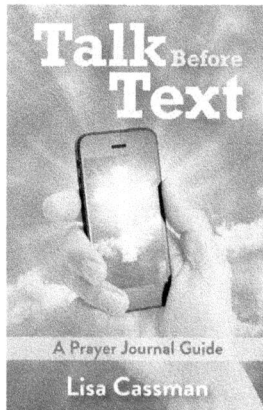

Talk Before Text: A Prayer Journal Guide
ISBN Paperback: 978-1-61244-777-3

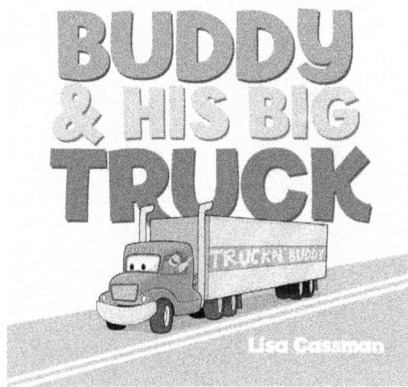

Buddy and His Big Truck
ISBN Hardcover: 978-1-63765-001-1
ISBN Paperback: 978-1-61244-991-3

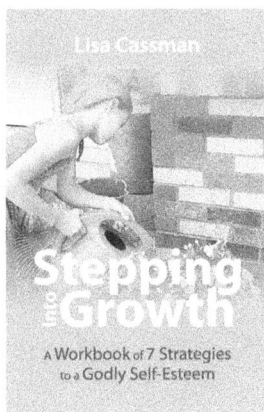

Stepping Into Growth: A Workbook
of 7 Strategies to a Godly Self-Esteem
ISBN Paperback: 978-1-63765-185-8

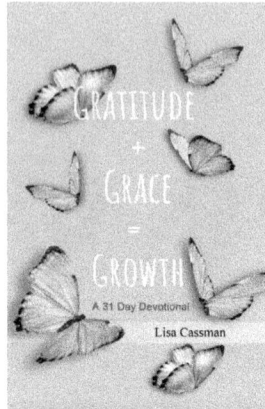

Gratitude + Grace = Growth: A 31-Day Devotional
A 31-day devotional to enrich your inner and outer life by creating space for gratitude and grace, thereby attending to your growth. There is more to this life than you yet know. Let Lisa guide you there.

AUTHOR • SPEAKER • PASTOR • LIFE COACH

## Let's Connect

Get to know Lisa Cassman

Website:
www.lisacassman.com
www.findingthebeautifulyou.com.

Facebook: www.facebook.com/lcassman

www.ingramcontent.com/pod-product-compliance
Lightning Source LLC
Chambersburg PA
CBHW052009090426

42741CB00008B/1613